D1224786

dabblelab

10-MINUTE
DRAWING
PROJECTS

BY CHRISTOPHER HARBO
ILLUSTRATED BY LUCY MAKUC

CAPSTONE PRESS
a capstone imprint

Dabble Lab is published by Capstone Press, an imprint of Capstone.
1710 Roe Crest Drive, North Mankato, Minnesota 56003
www.capstonepub.com

**Library of Congress Cataloging-in-Publication Data is available
on the Library of Congress website**
ISBN 978-1-4966-8089-1 (library binding)
ISBN 978-1-4966-8093-8 (eBook PDF)

Summary: Looking for quick and easy drawing projects for your
makerspace? Look no further! From kittens and race cars to aliens and
castles, these amazing 10-minute drawing projects will have kids making
in no time!

Design Elements
Shutterstock: Keport, Tukang Desain

Editorial Credits
Designer: Tracy McCabe; Media Researcher: Tracy Cummins; Production
Specialist: Katy LaVigne

All internet sites appearing in back matter were available and accurate
when this book was sent to press.

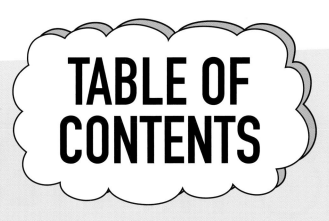

TABLE OF CONTENTS

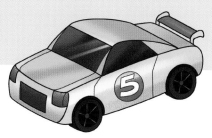

GOT 10 MINUTES?

What can you do with just 10 minutes to spare? Draw, of course! Just sharpen a pencil, grab a scrap of paper, and follow the simple step-by-step diagrams. In minutes, you'll have an amazing collection of animals, vehicles, monsters, and more!

General Supplies and Tools

colored pencils
erasers
paper
pencils
pencil sharpener

Tips

- Practice makes perfect! The more times you draw something, the better it will look.

- Sketch lightly at first and don't be afraid to make mistakes. Simply use an eraser to remove any unwanted lines.

- There's no right or wrong way to create art! Experiment and use your imagination.

- Change things up! Once you've mastered drawing the character one way, try drawing it in a different way.

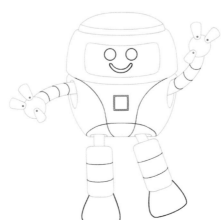

KITTEN

If you like drawing cats, you've come to the right place.
This curious kitty is as cute as a button!

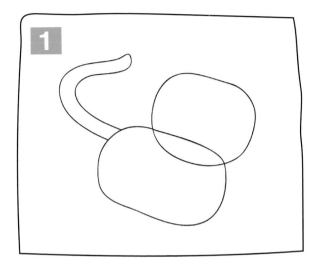

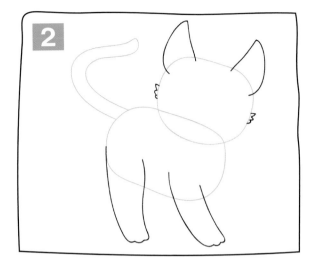

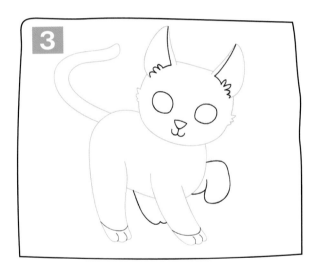

TIP Draw a collar, bow, or bell on your kitten to really make it your own.

PUPPY

If puppies are more your style, you're in luck.
This playful pooch will practically leap off the
page with a few simple steps.

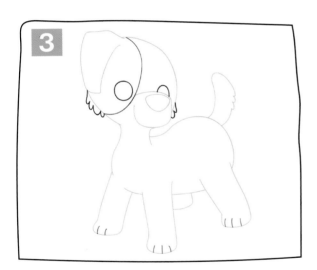

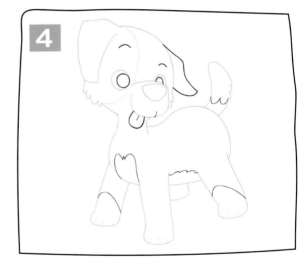

TIP Changing up your pup is simple. Just add a pattern or texture to her coat, such as spots, stripes, or curly hair!

PONY

What gets a pony prancing? A tasty treat of course! Draw this happy horse as it munches on a sweet, juicy apple!

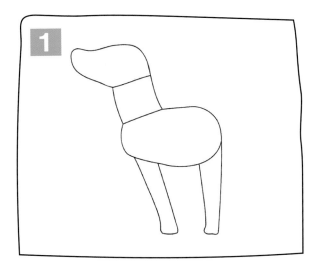

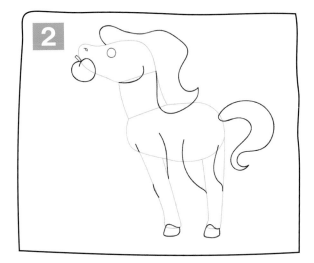

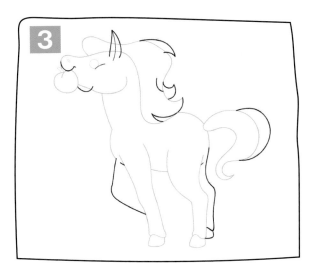

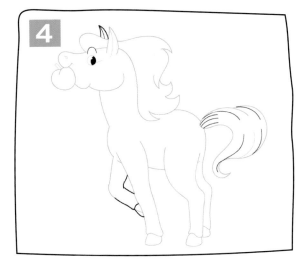

TIP Apples aren't the only things ponies like to snack on. Try switching out the apple with a carrot or a stalk of celery.

ANGELFISH

Glub, glub, glub. Go on an underwater adventure
by learning to draw this amazing angelfish!

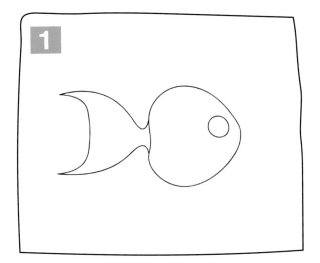

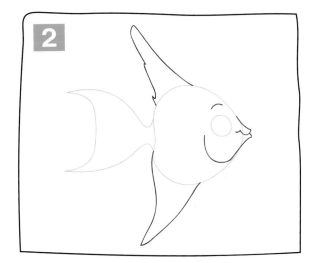

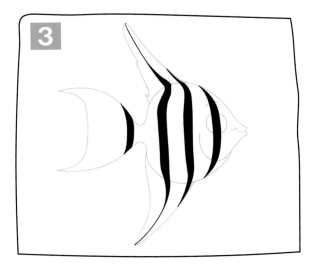

TIP Draw more types of fish by changing the size and shape of the angelfish's body. There's no limit to the kinds of fish you can create!

SPIDER

Don't let this little guy scare you. He may have eight hairy legs, but this super-simple spider is a cinch to draw.

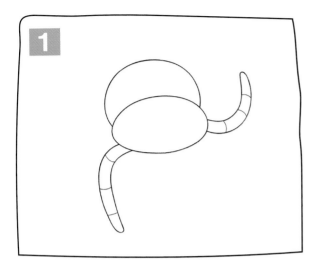

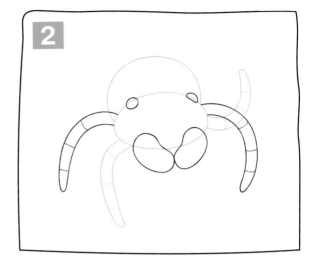

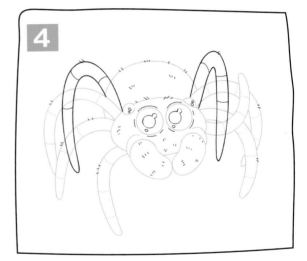

TIP Turn your tiny spider into a mutant monster. Just add mini houses, trees, and people around his legs to make him a towering titan!

ROBOT

One day, robots may help you do everything—even clean your room! Until that happens, test your art skills on this friendly bot.

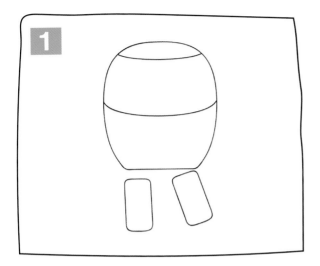

TIP Add a background that tells a story. Computer panels could show that your robot is on board a spacecraft. A junkyard could mean he's been tossed in the trash!

SPACE ALIEN

Greetings from the cosmos! Draw this friendly space alien as he waves hello from a passing asteroid.

TIP Draw one large alien and two smaller space aliens on either side of him. You'll create a whole space alien family!

MONSTER

Imagine you are hiking in the mountains without a camera when you cross paths with this monster. What are you going to do? Draw it, of course!

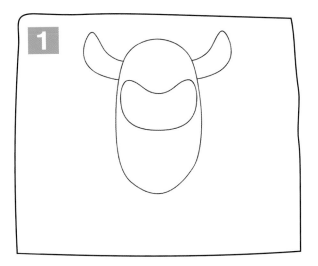

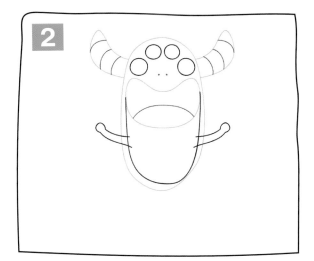

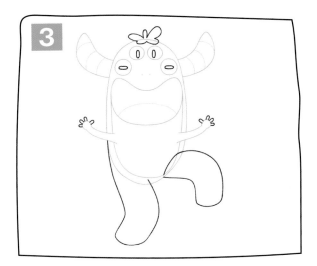

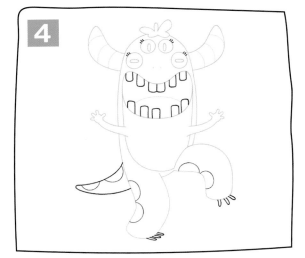

TIP Use your imagination to modify your monster! Add arms, legs, or even more heads to make it truly one of a kind.

RACE CAR

VROOM! VROOM! VROOM! Now's your chance to
draw the race car of your dreams. Just sharpen
your pencils and you'll be off to the races!

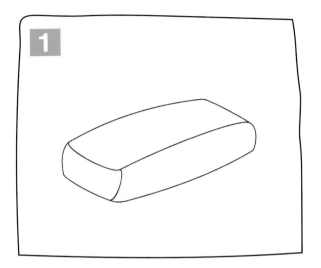

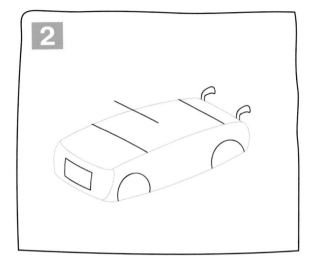

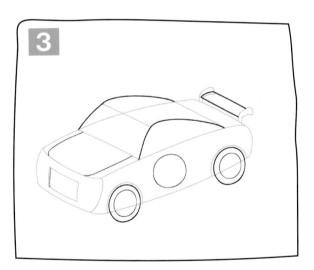

TIP Make your race car look like it is roaring down the track. Just add a few motion lines off the back of the car to give some ZOOM to its vroom!

JET

When it comes to drawing, it never hurts to set
your sights high. Do just that with a sleek jet
that glides through the clouds.

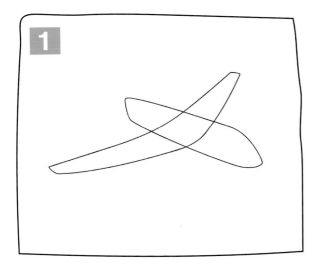

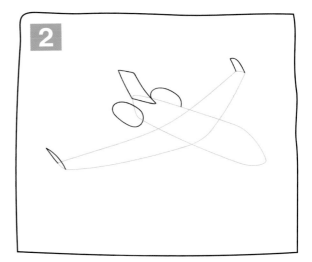

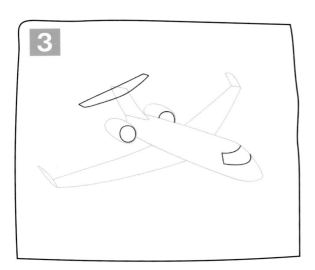

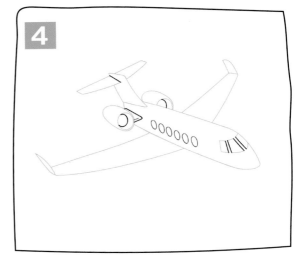

TIP Where in the world is your jet? Add a background, such as mountains or a famous landmark, to help tell a story.

SPACESHIP

3, 2, 1, blast off! Imagine yourself soaring through the solar system as you draw this simple spaceship.

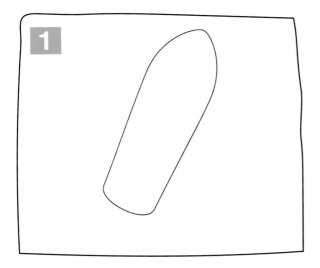

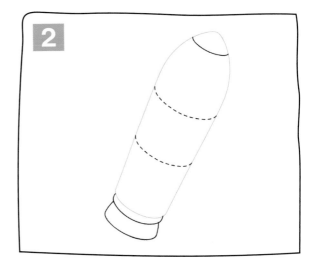

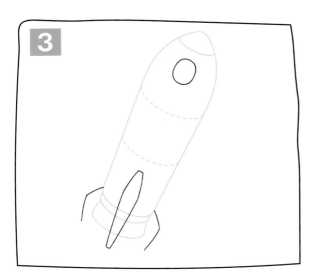

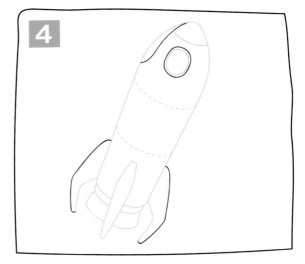

TIP Every spacecraft needs a pilot. Draw an astronaut or alien waving out the window. You decide!

SUNFLOWER

Need a quick way to brighten your day? Draw this
stunning sunflower in just 10 minutes or less!

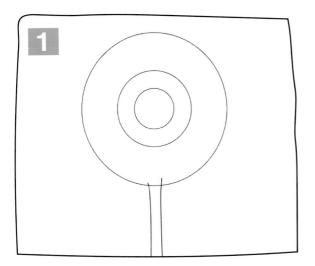

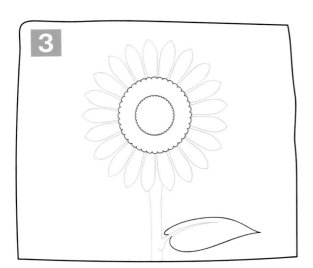

TIP Change the shape of the petals to create daisies, pansies, and other kinds of flowers.

CASTLE

Hear ye, hear ye! Test your skills by drawing a royal palace that would be perfect for any king or queen.

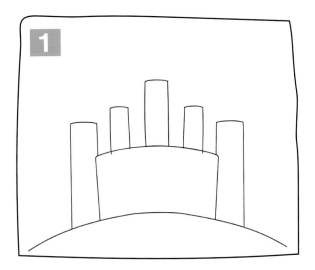

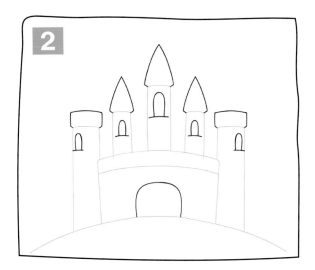

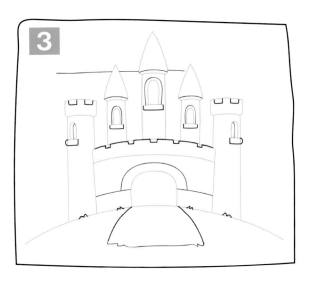

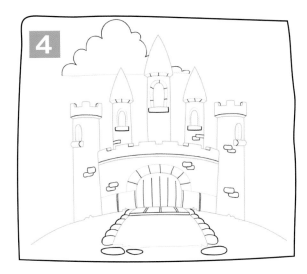

TIP Try adding extra details to your castle. Decorate the pointed towers with flags. Or add walls on the left and right to turn your castle into a fortress!

Read More

Bird, Benjamin. *Animal Doodles with Scooby-Doo!* North Mankato, MN: Capstone Press, 2017.

Bolte, Mari. *Draw Amazing Animal Mash-ups.* North Mankato, MN: Capstone Press, 2018.

Orgullo, Marisa. *I Want to Draw Dinosaurs.* New York: PowerKids Press, 2019.

Internet Sites

How to Draw Archives—Art for Kids
www.artforkidshub.com/how-to-draw

How to Draw—Drawing for Kids
www.hellokids.com/r_12/drawing-for-kids

How to Draw—Step by Step Drawing for Kids and Beginners
www.easypeasyandfun.com/how-to-draw